THE LITTLE BOOK OF SPICE TIPS

Al

THE LITTLE BOOK OF SPICE TIPS

ANDREW LANGLEY

Absolute Press

First published in Great Britain in 2006 by
Absolute Press, an imprint of Bloomsbury Publishing Plc
Scarborough House, 29 James Street West
Bath BA1 2BT, England
Phone +44 (0)1225 316013 **Fax** +44 (0)1225 445836
E-mail info@absolutepress.co.uk
Web www.absolutepress.co.uk

Reprinted 2013.

A catalogue record of this book is available from the British Library
ISBN: 9781904573487
Printed and bound by Hung Hing, China

Bloomsbury Publishing Plc
50 Bedford Square, London WC1B 3DP | www.bloomsbury.com

'Awake, O north wind; and come,
thou south; blow upon my garden,
that the spices thereof may flow out.'

Song of Solomon, 4:15

1

Buy your spices whole whenever possible, and grind and crush them when you need them. They will retain their aroma and potency much better this way – once ground, spices begin to lose theirs very quickly.

2

If you are going to use them immediately (within two or three hours), **buy ground spices.**

Try and get them from a specialist shop, where you know the stock will be reasonably fresh. Ground spices in packets could be months old.

3

Check through your store of spices at least once a month.

Make a note of essential items (such as chillies, cloves, pepper, paprika) which are running low. Chuck out any ground spices which were there when you last looked.

4

Most hard spices (pepper and coriander seed, for instance) **need to be ground up** so that they can release their flavour. This is best done with a ceramic pestle and mortar, or with a ball mill such as a 'flavour shaker'. An electric coffee grinder also does the job, though it will generate heat which can affect the aromas.

5

Treat spices with respect.

They contain chemicals which, in small quantities, will add exciting and magical flavours to food. But these same chemicals are actually toxic, and in large quantities can be very unpleasant. A grating of nutmeg adds a heavenly touch: a whole nutmeg may give you nasty hallucinations.

6

Store whole and ground spices **in jars with good airtight lids.** And keep the jars in a dry place well away from excess heat and light. Both can spoil the flavour of the spices.

7

Make sure you label (and date) your spice jars.

This is especially important when storing ground spices. Ground coriander seed and cumin can look very similar, as can ground cinnamon and allspice. Sniffing is not always the best way to judge – no-one wants a snootful of cayenne.

8

Improve the flavours of some spices by roasting before use. It also makes them more brittle and easier to grind. Heat a heavy frying pan (dry) and add the spices, shaking occasionally. About 3 minutes should do – don't burn them. This process is particularly good for seeds of cumin, fennel, mustard and sesame.

9

Hot oil can transform spices. It concentrates the characters of many kinds of spice, from cinnamon sticks, cloves and chillies to cumin seeds, cardamom pods and chopped ginger. Drop them in very hot groundnut oil or ghee (clarified and strained butter) before adding the rest of the ingredients for a dish.

10

Classic Spice Mix No.1: Quatre Epices.

The French use this combination to flavour stews and pâtés. It's called 'four spices', but usually contains at least five. Grind together a cinnamon stick, 10 cloves, a teaspoon of ground ginger, a good grating of nutmeg and 2 teaspoons of white peppercorns. You can also add a teaspoon of allspice.

11

Add a pinch of

freshly ground **cardamom**

seed **to your** freshly ground

coffee before brewing. It will give the brew an exciting edge. Cardamom works best with creamy coffee.

12

Despite the name, allspice is just one spice – although its flavour reminds you of several others. It used to be known as Jamaica pepper, because the best supplies come from that Caribbean island. **Cracked allspice berries work brilliantly in marinades for pork.**

13

Keep a vanilla pod or two in your sugar jar.

They will impart their own heavenly and delicate flavour to the sugar. You can use the same vanilla pods for infusing custards or syrups – then wash them and put them back in the sugar jar.

14

Paprika and caraway seeds are

the two spices essential to porkolt,

the great dish of Hungary. Mix 25g (1oz) of paprika (mild rose if possible) with frying onions, then put in 1kg (2.2lb) of lean stewing beef and a little water. Add 1 teaspoon of caraway seeds, salt and a slosh of vinegar. Cover tightly and stew gently for an hour.

15

Classic Spice Mix No.2: Chermoula.

This Moroccan mixture makes a superb marinade for fish. Blend together a teaspoon of hot paprika, a big pinch of ground cumin, a more modest pinch of cayenne, bunches of chopped parsley and coriander leaves, 5 garlic cloves, vinegar, lemon juice and salt.

16

Harissa is a very hot chilli paste used widely in North Africa.

Make your own by soaking 30g (1oz) of red chillies in hot water for an hour, then draining, chopping and pounding them with 2 cloves of garlic and a little salt. Put in a jar and cover with olive oil. A thin outer coating of harissa produces a startling new dimension to roast chicken.

17

Saffron threads may look thin and unimpressive, but they **add both stunning colour and delicate aromas.** Get the best out of them by soaking in a little hot water or milk and using this liquid in cooking – especially fish stew and paella.

18

Lemon grass lives up to its name perfectly,

with its fresh lemony flavour and stalky appearance. The stalks can be hard to pulp, however. Cut off the lumpy knot at the bottom and pound them lightly before slicing thinly. Then the food processor can cope more easily.

19

Certain spices have achieved miracle-working status. **Nectar des Dieux,** the spiced spirit of Southern France, is said to be the secret **for a long life.**

Steep tablespoons of coriander seed and aniseed, 4 cloves and a cinnamon stick in 300ml ($^1/_2$ pint) of eau-de-vie or vodka. A month later add 150ml ($^1/_4$ pint) of sugary syrup, mixed with 300ml ($^1/_2$ pint) of white wine. Strain, cork and leave for three months.

20

Classic Spice Mix No.3: Garam Masala.

The famous aromatic mixture of North India and Pakistan has many variations, but it's always best to make your own. This is a basic version. Grind together half a cinnamon stick, 1 teaspoon each of cloves, black peppercorns and cumin seeds, 1 tablespoon of cardamom seeds and a good grating of nutmeg.

21

Always buy nutmegs whole.

Keep them in a jar with their own little grater, so that it won't get lost. If you are grinding a spice mixture which needs a chunk of nutmeg, simply bash the whole nut lightly with a hammer or rolling pin and it will fall to pieces.

22

Preserved lemons are a

a key ingredient in many **Moroccan and Greek meat dishes.**

Soak 6 lemons in warm water for 3 days, changing the water daily. Slice the lemons (discarding ends and pips) and layer them in a jar with salt and a mixture of coriander seeds, cloves, peppercorns and cinnamon fragments. Top up with fresh lemon juice, seal and eat after a month.

23

When using a small amount of fresh ginger,

peel and grate while it is still attached to the main chunk.

If you cut off a small piece and grate that, you'll end up with ragged finger ends. Grated fresh ginger features in many recipes from the Far East.

24

Lemon and mustard seed chutney

makes the most of the nutty tang of whole mustard. Thinly slice 4 onions and 4 lemons, sprinkle with salt and leave overnight. Then add 500ml (16 fl oz) of white wine vinegar, 1 teaspoon of ground allspice, 2 of mustard seed, 500g (1lb 2oz) of sugar and 120g (4oz) of raisins. Simmer for 45 minutes and put in jars when cool.

25

Classic Spice Mix No.3: Chinese Five-Spice.

Put together a tablespoon of Sichuan peppercorns, a tablespoon of fennel seed, 2 teaspoons of cloves, 4 whole star anise and half a cinnamon stick. Grind finely. This famous mixture is used for marinating meat and poultry before stewing or grilling.

26

Many spices can be infused to make refreshing tisanes.

One of the best features fennel seed. Boil 1 teaspoon of seeds in a cup of water for 5 minutes. Strain before drinking.

27

Chilli and vodka is a sensational combination.

Vodka is drunk cold, while chillies are hot. Simply stick 4 or 5 chillies plus 10 juniper berries in bottle of good vodka and leave for a month. Drink exceedingly well chilled.

28

Get rid of the seeds and veins of chillies

– dried or fresh – before chopping or grinding. The seeds, especially, can add too much hotness to a dish and overwhelm the other flavours. Tear open the pods, pull off the veins and shake out the seeds.

29

When chopping chillies, always be sure to **wash your hands thoroughly afterwards.**

This spice is incredibly powerful. You won't feel its sting on your fingers, but if you accidentally rub your eyes or your lips with unwashed hands, you'll be sorry. Alternatively, wear kitchen gloves.

30

Make your own *nam prik pow.*

It is a chilli paste from Thailand with a thousand uses – great for adding richness and spice to your dishes. Chop and sauté together 3 red chillies, 3 shallots and 3 garlic cloves until they're soft. Stir in a tablespoon each of sugar and tamarind concentrate together with a little water. It should have the consistency of jam. Seal in a jar and keep in the fridge.

31

Make your own beautiful red chilli oil. Fill a (warmed) storage jar about one third full with dried chillies. Heat sunflower or groundnut oil and pour into the jar. Seal tightly and leave for a month. Strain at least twice through muslin to get the fully translucent colour.

32

Fennel seeds go stunningly well with belly of pork. Take a 1.5kg (3lb 5oz) chunk of good pork belly, score the skin side thoroughly with a sharp knife and salt it. Cover the flesh side with a mixture of fennel seeds and crushed garlic and leave for an hour. Roast at blistering heat for 30 minutes, then at low heat for another 2 hours.

33

This Indian green vegetable soup is a riot of spicy contrasts.

Simmer 2 diced potatoes and a chopped onion in chicken stock with some peeled ginger, 1 teaspoon of ground coriander and 2 teaspoons of ground cumin. After 30 minutes, add a packet of frozen peas, a chopped green chilli, the juice of a lemon, and a teaspoon of ground roasted cumin. Whizz in the blender and stir in a little cream.

34

Fresh mango is **heavenly**

enough, but **fresh**

mango relish

is even better. Roughly blend together two peeled and chopped mangoes, half a sliced red onion, a chunk of grated ginger, a chopped chilli, chopped coriander leaves and the juice of one lime or half a lemon. Let stand for 30 minutes before serving.

35

Try a variation on steak au poivre – steak au coriandre.

Grind up 1 tablespoon of coriander seed, 1 tablespoon of black peppercorns and a large pinch of salt. Coat both sides of some good sirloin steak with the mixture and leave for two hours. Grill or fry in groundnut oil – but not for too long.

36

Give a new dimension to roast potatoes

by cooking them with crushed juniper berries. This works best with small, whole, newish potatoes. Heat vegetable oil in a roasting dish and add a handful of juniper berries lightly bashed in a pestle. Then bung in the potatoes (make sure they get coated in the oil) and roast for 30 minutes or so.

37

Be sparing with cloves in cooking. They are surprisingly powerful – try holding one on your tongue for a minute or two – and can easily blank out other tastes. Stick no more than six (three is even better) into the onion when flavouring stocks, stews or bread sauce.

38

This is **a great spicy onion chutney**

that goes with almost any kind of meat course in Indian cooking. And it takes almost no time to prepare. Slice an onion into wafer-thin rings. Toss in a bowl with salt, the juice of half a lemon, a big pinch of hot paprika and a small pinch of cayenne pepper. Leave for 30 minutes before using.

39

Cardamom and beetroot make a magical pairing. This recipe was popular in Victorian times. Bake four large beetroot very gently for 2 to 3 hours. Cool, peel and slice thinly. Then sprinkle them with sugar, salt and 2 teaspoons of ground cardamom seed. Moisten with a vinaigrette and serve well chilled.

40

Aniseed works wonders on your stomach.

It is famous in many cultures for aiding digestion, sweetening the breath and curing flatulence. You can chew the seeds, or make a tisane by steeping a tablespoon of aniseed in 1 litre (2 pints) of boiling water for 5 minutes. Strain, cool and drink a full glass twice a day.

41

Spices for pickling: an all-purpose mix. If you're doing a big batch of pickling, you'll need a good quantity of spiced vinegar. Mix one tablespoon each of allspice, cloves, mustard seed, black peppercorns and coriander seed, 3 chillies and a chunk of ginger root. Crush lightly and boil up briefly in 4 litres (8 pints) of cider vinegar with 225g (8oz) of brown sugar. Allow to cool before using.

42

For particularly pleasing pickles, use single spices

instead of many. Each spice highlights a different flavour in individual fruits or vegetables. For instance, try cardamom with peaches or pears, coriander seed with quinces, dill seed with cucumbers and white peppercorns with walnuts.

43

Spices for mulling wine: a German Christmas mix.

It's easy to go wild with spices and lose identifiable flavours. This recipe needs only 2 cinnamon sticks and 6 cloves. Simmer for 5 minutes with a cup of water, orange and lemon rind and 175g (6oz) white sugar. Then heat this up with a bottle each of white and red wine and a big slug of brandy.

44

Treasure your supply of turmeric. It has countless uses – from dyeing the robes of Buddhist monks to taking centre stage in most curry powders and masalas. Turmeric is also celebrated as an antiseptic. Mix powdered turmeric into a paste with lime juice to anoint skin ulcers and other sores.

45

Fight colds and sore throats with spices.

Briefly simmer a cinnamon stick and 4 cloves in 500ml (1pint) of water. Strain and mix in the juice of half a lemon, 2 teaspoons of honey and a stiff tot of Irish whiskey.

46

Sesame seeds are a rich source of vitamins and minerals. Toast them lightly and sprinkle over salads and cooked vegetables. They go sensationally well with a mix of thinly sliced carrots and courgettes which have been sautéed in olive oil (better still, sesame oil).

47

Grind black peppercorns over sliced strawberries.

This surprising combination brings out the best in both ingredients and creates a refreshing breakfast starter. Squeeze some orange juice over the fruit first for added bite.

48

Capers are an essential ingredient of tapenade, that most addictive of all spreads. In a processor, blend together 100g (4oz) of pitted black olives, two anchovy fillets and a tablespoon of rinsed capers. Drizzle in olive oil and lemon juice until you get the consistency that suits. Optional extra: a dash of Dijon mustard.

49

Liquorice adds body and earthy sweetness **to slow-cooked beef.** Pop two or three small chunks of liquorice root into the casserole with the stock and other flavourings. Remember to take them out before serving.

50

Use asafoetida very sparingly.

It smells horrible, and has a powerful taste. Bought ground, it must be kept in a tightly-sealed container. All the same, a pinch of asafoetida subtly enhances grilled fish and vegetables. It's an intriguing substitute for garlic.

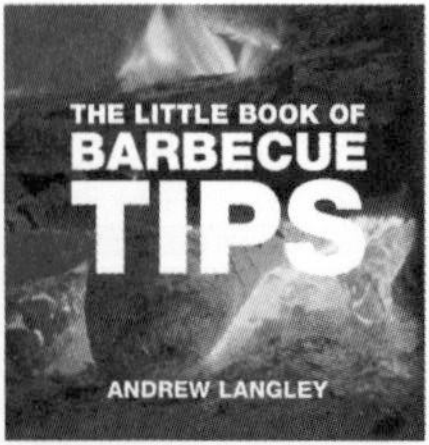
THE LITTLE BOOK OF
BARBECUE
TIPS
ANDREW LANGLEY

THE LITTLE BOOK OF
BEER
TIPS
ANDREW LANGLEY

THE LITTLE BOOK OF
HERB
TIPS
WILLIAM FORTT

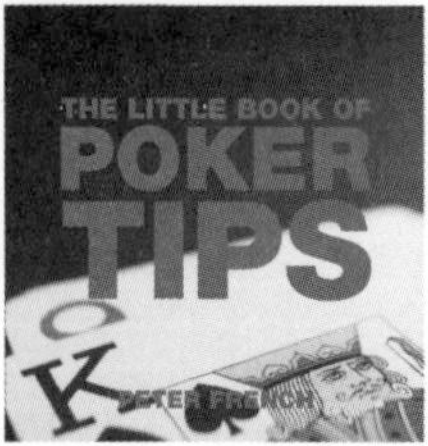
THE LITTLE BOOK OF
POKER
TIPS
PETER FRENCH

THE LITTLE BOOK OF
GARDENING
TIPS
WILLIAM FORTT

THE LITTLE BOOK OF
CHEFS'
TIPS
RICHARD MAGGS

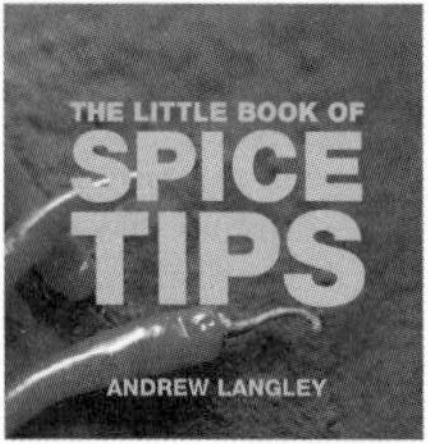
THE LITTLE BOOK OF
SPICE
TIPS
ANDREW LANGLEY

THE LITTLE BOOK OF
GOLF
TIPS
PETER FRENCH

THE LITTLE BOOK OF
TIPS
SERIES